Pape,

hopeless
dangerous
lonely
bored
scared
trapped
abandoned
love
friendless
sad
mad
bad

Feelings drip
onto these pages
of poems written by
youth participating in
a program sponsored by
Do The *Write* Thing of DC.

Contents

What is the What?

Haiku & Clerihew

Foreword

Paper Outlets is a product of some of the most gifted youth from the heart of the nation's capital. This unique collection reflects true brilliance.

Do The *Write* Thing of DC was specifically established to teach youth how to write and publish their own work.

As the Executive Director, witnessing these youth transform into young publishers through copyediting and marketing was simply enthralling. While engaged in the creative process, these young masters of verse displayed an amazing and insightful depth of knowledge. Intense, performance-based workshops enhanced the flow of their artistic energies, and what can only be described as an explosion of mental supernovae burst forward into consciousness.

With a perspective unrivaled by any other American city, they tapped into the spirit of their wisdom, living life in the District during an unprecedented time in our country's storied history. For them to be here, present, bathed in the power of knowing our city is home to the first Black American President, it was the perfect backdrop for their ruminations to spring to life.

In these pages allow these poets to take you on a transcendent journey into their thoughts and feel what it means to Do The *Write* Thing!

Look forward,

Gerald Nordé
Executive Director
Do The *Write* Thing of DC

Introductory Note

It is harder than one might think to ignite a fire. To create sparks so minute and dazzling while providing ample space to allow them to develop into gorgeous depictions of scarlet and sun-kissed silhouettes dancing and intertwining amongst the molecules of our atmosphere. We are the shadows of these flames overlooked yet prancing just the same. Forced to burn our emotions onto parchment used as an outlet spewing energy formed from a re-useable resource little of the world knows exists. So use this book as a guide, a traveler's tool if you will, that inspires you to communicate and tell people how you really feel.

Ava McCoy
12th Grade
Program Assistant

Black Flames

Catch the fire in poems by DC Public School students participating in a program sponsored by Do The Write *Thing of DC.*

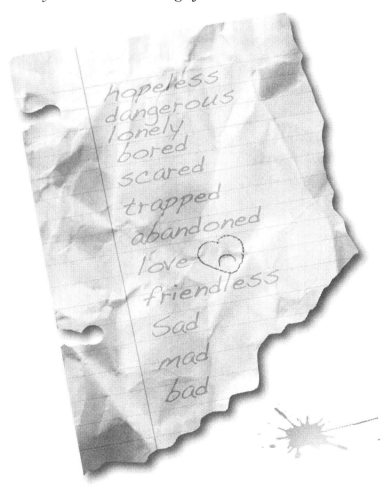

HIP HOP HIP HOP
Nadja Theodore

Hip Hop Hip Hop
It all started in the Bronx
Biggie Smalls and Tupac helped make hip hop
With the slick rhymes and big beats to the
Poetry and Beat box

Hip Hop Hip Hop
Rappers today think that hip hop
Is just about rapping words
And singing songs
Niki Minaj should just make a
Rap about Ping Pongs
And she would still make millions
Off a stupid rap song

Hip Hop Hip Hop
If you listen to what they are saying
You'd be like "Man they just playing"
Always rapping about girls and having sex
Never about children without homes
That need to be blessed
Man, rappers today
Are just a mess

Hip Hop Hip Hop
But you see I'm the hypocrite
I know all of the words to every Niki Minaj
and Lil Wayne song

Continued

HIP HOP HIP HOP *(continued)*

But my poem is not here to put any one down
But look at you
You look like a clown
Mouth full of gold
Pockets full of cash
You ain't helping no one
You really think you're first class??
You should just stop
While you are ahead
Filling our heads with all of this gore
Man this ain't even HIP HOP anymore!!!

LET IT GO

Sherman Davis

as i sit back and rest
i look at a tree
there's a nest
the mother's blessed

I'm here just at rest
tired from all the stress
it's all in my chest
medicine won't help much
toxins flowing through
my very veins

as i try to get up
i just flop back
this seat filled with
tears is all i know now

as i look up and out
to look at the blue
with no doubts
i have to open the hatch

express and light the match
and ignite the fire inside
and in that way
everything will go
AWAYYYYYYYY

LET IT GO - PART 2
Sherman Davis

as i stand
i look about
i take a stride
without a doubt

i had to pout
then i started to shout
just to let it all out
it won't go away
it needs
to be
far as the eye
can see

i strain myself
just to deal with it
to suppress the flame
not to ignite it

grabbed the fire extinguisher.
put it out quick
never ever knew
that it be difficult
to keep it inside

built up walls
never let anybody inside
these walls are paper thin

in these walls i reside in
i sleep the days away
wondering about
passing through my walls
except the last one

change of heart
no heart test exact
but i think
i had a heart attack
i'm clear just been brought back

now i lay on my bed
just on my back
as i drift off into dream land.
i snap back & look out the window
i thought the birds said
let the stress go out the window!

SITTING IN THE DARK KICKING
   Sherman Davis

as i lay my head on the floor
i wonder
i take in the world
cold harsh unforgiving
never to get a chance

i've seen things
known things
even heard things
i've never fathomed in my brain

it all makes sense
in some lessons
but chapters
can't hear
can't read
can't learn

i look around
i wonder
who's there
now and later
cuz I'm scared

but no one paid their dues
so i have no spectators
I'm tired of it all
crying

headaches
the pain
the regret
the losses
the tears
the scares
everything

i just try to hide it inside
until i can die with it
just trying to give you something
i can't even provide

i look around
the darkness creeps up
and surrounds me
no exits
no where to go
this is the end

darkness engulfed me
I'm dead to the world
even within
i've died in the darkness
of everything

but all that remains is me
and my will sheathed
inside my determined body
all i'm doing is sitting in darkness kicking
but in the end i know i won't get any......"H.E.L.P"

I'M JUST ME!

Sherman Davis

i'm just me, that's all i can be, just me
i'll never be what you want me to be
i'm not a doll, i'm surely not a barbie
i can't pose for the camera, let me do me

i'm not walking the way you are
my walk is for me, not for others to copy
why can't people see me for me, not just an image
i'm not a mirror so what you see
is not you, it's me
it's always been me

if you wanna have a copy go find someone else
if you think you can have another that acts like me
it ain't going to fly
i'm the ORIGINAL

i can do a lot of things that the wannabes can't do
i can flip, i can write poetry, i can do a lot of things
hell i even read
most black kids don't even like to read
and that's just sad to me.

now let's get back to the starting point of this whole thing
I'M JUST ME!!!!

FAST ROAD TO RECOVERY!!
Sherman Davis

i'm on a stretcher, i just got a sickness
all this bacteria, it's eating away at my ears
and spread to my heart that's so-o-o so-o dear
where's my doc at with the health packs

it's 12 o'clock, i haven't even slept a day
i'm stuck here in this chair with a worried brain
and pain from the center of my veins
where's my superwomen; i don't have one
i just wish i could cry and maybe there could be one

i don't understand where it is
i'm tired of just knowing but not seeing
there's a pain in my chest that just won't stop
it'll hurt but it'll stop just as i drop
oh no my heart stopped, i'm dead

three hours pass
i just woke up
i look to my right
the doctor's there and he says to me
YOU'RE ON YOUR WAY TO A FAST RECOVERY

THE DREAM
Sherman Davis

i've been through it all up to being a man there ain't nothin i
ain't seen yet you should get a blues clue instead of a red clue
i need a bandaid because i fell head first don't cry i just want a
nurse because all my pain is oozing from my right arm back into
my veins yea you can see the pain of a youngster now when
the years go by i'm back in the E.R. again i'll be a little bit older
then will it be different none the less i just hope i can get free
from this seat i'm tied down just kicking i've tried to get untied
but the suicide is just too sublime i've grown to know taking a
life is a big mistake there's a butterfly next to me i look at and
all i wanna do is just think about don't wanna express plane to
salvation let me marinate in the pain a bit so i can boil it into
happiness my eyes are white that's all the tears that have come
from years of turning gears that's inside the years of my youth
into adulthood maybe there's something i should look forward
to is this it for me? my revelation of my upbringing i dont know
but i'll try to find out someone pinch me see if i can wake up
cuz right now i'm in a deep sleep something like hibernation but
there's no end to this state i can't awake from this nightmarish
sleep it's stuck on re re re re re re re pe pe pe pe peat please
someone anyone this is madness can't you see i have a twisted
mind so when i wake up again...
WHO Am I........ DOCTOR ....HE HAD THE DREAM AGAIN

DAYS GO BY
By Sherman Davis

here and there a day goes by and none of them i lived to the fullest i wonder if i could rewind time to the point of 12 and 9 now that time is nonexistent but so are my eyes nonexistent in time there's always a reason why people say i wish it was more time just so i could spend more time with you and until the end of time there's something else between the avenue of time and space there's a clock that keeps the pace between the space but we all watch as time is waste just like toxic gas we sufficate as i stare at the sun i say to myself days go by

IT TAKES
By Sherman Davis

it's just everything that we do it takes everything where it all begins from the heart and through the veins again people push themselves every day of the week there's more energy in the world than any breathing thing that stands it takes more to know that the world is our oyster and we're the pearls that reside within it's going to take a miracle to realize that there's a will left to us but we just can't see what it is because we're too blind to see what's a lie so we just say a whole bunch of words that have no meaning which means it's half-baked not even ready to be served maybe there might be a day when it takes all the strength inside to make one mystery that couldn't be solved put in the light to let the darkness leak out of it and let the light shine behind it.........it takes belief!

A YO!
By Sherman Davis

a yo who me yea you right there on the corner what's your philosophy what's your meaning for selling drugs what's the cash for buddy is there blood on that cash or is it just dirty money will you ever wake up from this devilish dream

won't you step into the light with just no regrets just honesty yes i know it's hard to do good but it's hard to do bad as well going home to a mother of nine it's hard to feed little kids that are all under ten

every night you pray to god to wake up like it used to be with smiles and no pain no stabs no bullet holes a car and a key to start the engine no cops that parade through the house to find a treasure that's not there walking around your house with no map

what happens if i told you if you make the right decisions that you'll have the best outcome and good income yea there's taxes to be paid but they will come back to you but with more riches because nobody died from even telling you the truth

sometimes things that people say that are good other people picture it as a dream maybe you gotta do the right thing to step out of that frame yea life is a picture but you choose what the painting will be maybe you can start off with just one halo and two wings and listen to the big man that had a lot to do with your upbringing

i wish there was something i could say to make a person turn their head and stare but i'm just a kid who cares well men and women you use to be infants then kids then teens and then adults don't ever say grow up because you know you wanna become demoted in age instead of years you wanna go back

into those years when candy was the answer to most kids' ears
and video games were played everywhere

sometimes i don't wanna grow up but i have to so you should
do the same before life tames you you'll be sorry for not reading
this poem because what i write are Deep thoughtZ but my
words are in the pot they are just too hot to the touch but they're
not hot once you can blow on it and taste it with the tip of your
tongue and you can finally see without being mad at what you
just heard

yea some people call me a goody goody but i call myself a king
someone that knows the right thing from the bad things yea it's
so good to be bad but it's over achieving to do good but that's a
medal and a rocket that blasts you off into space i don't need to
be under the influence because i'm in outer space I'll be darn if
i'm under the waves when i should be on a board surfing those
waves

(sleeping)...(wakes up)...oh man where am i looks over and sees
a kid at the corner on a dark night........A YO!

WHY MY LIFE?
Sherman Davis

Everywhere I turn all I see is sorrow
I'm tired of just wading in a pool of depression
And always wondering why I'm there
And I can't get out
How come people see me drowning
But never ever come to my aid when I need help
Its gets so hard to breath
I just went under
I'm choking because my life is like a ocean
I just gotta keep swimming and swimming
I can't stop or I'll drown in the ocean of tears and screams
I can't take it anymore
I'm tired of kicking and screaming
I'm tired of yelling and wanting
Won't somebody anybody help me please
Save me from this misery you call a mother please
Why do I have to stroll here and there for her
Why do I have to pretend like she's the perfect mom in the
world
But behind closed doors I know the real truth
I know what she does
Everything is not what it seems
I'm tired of lying
Why can't I just pass it on to someone else
Like a virus or like an infection
Just give it to everybody

Then they'll feel my pain everyday
Maybe when they feel how I feel
Maybe they'll help me
I just want to cry sooo badly
I just fight back the rain of tears
Just want to let it pour down to the hard ground below
Oh please God just take this burden away
Please just wipe it clean
Make it go away
Why shoulder your son with this burden
What can I prove from this
It's killing me inside and out
There is no bliss...it's just....I wanna ask....why my life??????????

OTHERS' EXPECTATIONS
By Evadne Lewis

I think back and laugh about the results of trying to put me and
you together
Our physical appearance together made me think we would last
forever
But when I realized I was being played like a game
I decided to play along with your bootlegged version of
monopoly
It's like when the so called best friend left
A boy's underarms after gym class is what you attempted
to make the sleeve of my shirt smell like
So I played my role and told you what you wanted to hear
But when it came down to getting what you wanted
It's like I learned from the best
When it came to meeting other's expectations

YOU'RE NOT ME...
Evadne Lewis

I hate it when you come for me acting as if you know everything
I hate when you say I can't do that
Or I shouldn't do this
There's a difference between this and that
There's a difference between what you think and what you know
There's a difference between what's right and wrong
There's a difference between what is said and what is done
And I think that I know, that this is not wrong but right, when I say that
You're not me...

LIVING ON THE EDGE
Maya Davenport

Love your strongest
Smile your longest
When you're down
Think of joyous moments
Laugh with friends
Stay up all night
Sometimes life must be lived
Without thinking twice

WITHOUT YOU
Maya Davenport

Every night I lay wondering what tomorrow has in store for me
Knowing that on the surface I'll be wearing a smile
But deep down my soul will be desperately shouting
Shouting for ears that will listen
Arms that will hold my heavy heart
Eyes that will care
And if I'm lucky a heart that will heal
Just another human being can have such a tremendous impact
It's amazing that without that person you feel like nothing
The feeling is breath taking
Everyday I feel myself fade a little
Soon I'll be gone

ALL BLACK GIRLS AREN'T LOUD
Ayanna Shingler

My voice wasn't made to stir up a crowd
I'm not that bold and sometimes my head hangs down
Because despite what you heard,
all black girls aren't LOUD
The volume of my voice don't fill a room
I keep to myself and quietly hum my own tune
Don't get me wrong I don't have low self-esteem,
I'm black, I'm proud
I'm just saying not all black girls are LOUD

LIFE
Lachelle Davis

Life is like a rock when you suffer the hard times of
your family.
They always get you into trouble
Feel like a dog chasing its tail
On the trail of this life, feels like a trail to the
Underground Railroad.
No water; no breeze

TRAPPED
Maya Davenport

No way to escape
hope has faded, lost all faith.
Innocent man locked away.
Not sure if he will see another day,
his three year old daughter.
What he'd do to hold her once more,
can't even wish her happy birthday
the constant tears make his eyes sore.
He writes letters to his daughter and wife
just in case he doesn't make it alive.
About how he loves them.
That he's sincerely tried.
Weak as can be on his bed he lays
doesn't even have the strength to pray.
Closes his eyes. Sees a light. Realizes
it's them leaning in to give him a kiss
as his daughter whispers—
"Daddy you will be missed."
They disappear leaving him alone.
He lets himself free, says
"It's time to go home."

MY LONG NIGHT
Vasco Whisenton

It was a long night
cold, streets full of
fog. Across the street
a cat or dog. Should I
run. Should I hide. I
cannot decide. I know.
Call a ride. Down the street
something big walking to me.
Running out of time.
Oh good. Oh good.
Here come the dog man.
Oh no there goes the dog.
The dog man running my way.
You going to help me I say.
The big dog biting at my feet.
Blood on my feet. Walking home
with blood on my feet.

LIVE FOR YOU
Maya Davenport

No one knows the true definition of life
Is it being savage and demented
Or maybe well thought out and careful
Should life be dedicated to a higher being
Or yourself alone
Whether you cherish life
Or live by the moment
Learn from mistakes
Have no regrets
Grow a little each day
It's your life
Live it your way

STOP THE VIOLENCE
Kiare Ford

At night when the killers come out
Where bullets act as flowers sprout
Where murderers kill kids and make families pout
Where people get hardwork and dull brains through
the snout.
At night where I lay
Where a 9 or a 40 can spray
Where hot slugs act as venom entering bodies
everyday
not only in DC but all around the USA.

NO PLACE TO CALL HOME
Shaynese Green

At night where I
lay sometimes I
don't want to stay
with nowhere to go
stand on my own
trying to be strong
no family by my side
I cry day and night
asking why
why me why can't I find
a happy home and a
family that loves me.

WHERE I'M FROM
Nicholas Moses

I'm from the hands of a hard working dad and a
loving, devoted mother
I'm from a two bedroom, brick house where two
parents and one brother live
I'm from POP! Don't Touch That!
I'm from sweet potatoes and baked chicken
I'm from air conditioning blowing like a winter breeze
I'm now from loneliness and quietness
I'm now from a place where positivity is at war with
negativity
And I'm not sure what side I should take or what
role I should play
They say your background tells a lot about you and
who/where you come from
Young people are often told chase your dreams,
don't let them chase you

MY MUSIC
Rebekah Newby

I like rock, metal, psychedelic and some hip-hop
I don't like R&B
It's just not me
I don't like go-go
Even though I live in DC
My friends call me "white"
I smile but I don't like it
All black people don't like R n B
All black people aren't fans of Lil' Wayne
And Young Money
I think they suck, that's just my opinion
I prefer MGMT, N.E.R.D, Asking Alexandria, and
Enter Shikari
I prefer Odd Future and
Tyler the Creator
And Pac Div's
"Running for Mayor"

PRAISE SONG FOR MUSIC

Nicholas Moses

Each day we blast our iPods
Bobbing our heads
Not caring what people think
We live from radio to iPod
Song to song
We encounter each other in a rap
Or in a bible hymn
"Yes, Jesus loves me"
All about us is positive music
That pushes us forward
Someone is hoping
for that shot at fame
Someone is trying
to make his talents seen or heard
A woman and her son are doing a duet
Of love, wisdom and courage
I know that tomorrow isn't promised
But don't shut down
Keep going; move ahead of your goals
Music is band
Cymbals clapping
Children's feet moving to the beats
Blues is gray skies
Rap is red fire burning through the day
Classical is blue waves
Jazz is golden trombones dancing
Country is brown dirt roads

(Continued)

PRAISE SONG FOR MUSIC *(continued)*

Say it plain: music is my passion
I shall see and hear
The drummers drumming
Praise song for the trumpets triumph
Say it plain: articulate
Praise song for each tap every beat
And every Wiz Khalifa
Some live by speakers bumping
and old folks thumping
Praise song for music

DREAMS
Darius Brown

When a person dreams
about making it into the pro's
or being a rapper people try to
crush his dreams, say
you won't make it past high school
but he does.
Now he's on his way to college.
To the Pro's.
Why in this world don't people
want to see a Black man make it in life.
Try to hold us back.

I WONDER
Tamesha Oden

Am I fat?
When
I walk down the street do
people notice me?
When I'm asleep
does my mother just stare at me?
When I eat do I look like
a homeless person who hasn't
eaten in ages?
If I
don't eat will that help me
lose weight?
Thinking No that's crazy!
I don't care what nobody thinks.
I'm Beautiful the way I am.
Like Dr. Suess says Sam I Am.
Beautiful Yes I Am.

STEREOTYPES
Dysis Scarlett

All black people
are not loud,
"ghetto."
Yes some
are more vocal
outspoken.
Technically "the ghetto"
is where people live.
Ghetto is not an adjective,
therefore it can't describe a person.

ALL BLACK PEOPLE CAN'T HAVE GOOD HAIR
Lashae Hunter

What makes them say that?
My sister is 100% black and she has good hair.
I'm trying to figure out why people say that.
What's the definition of good/pretty hair
if you're Black?

BLACKS ARE NOT GHETTO
Maya Davenport

All blacks are not ghetto.
Aren't always making the noise.
Aren't all addicted to drugs.
Starting the trouble.
Stop looking down on us.
Stop thinking you're on a higher level.
Don't judge.
Don't treat us like trash.
Remember the one that made a change.
They're one of a kind.
Keep that in mind.

JOHN
Daquan Lane

Wakes
Bakes
then
takes
cakes
rebakes
then
lays
down
for
the
day

ALL BLACK PEOPLE
Terrence Henderson

like chocolate
love chicken
like kool-aid
love Mc Donalds
ain't black
ain't racist
can do hair
love sports
are people.

THERE'S NO SUCH THING AS 'BLACK PEOPLE'S MUSIC'

Akayla Bracey

They say listen to your own music,
But what does that mean?
I have to blend in like a brown jellybean?
I can't "rock out" or scream really loud?
I can't embrace my originality or even be proud?
Why follow the rules; why be the same
When you can be the first to change up the game?
There's no shame,
You're not lame
No feeling to be the one you tame,
That came,
From fame
But once you aim to be different
They'll talk,
They'll sneer,
So why say I'm weird because I don't listen to music
that's black?
When did anyone even decide that?

ALL PEOPLE ARE THE SAME?

Terry Daniels

All black boys don't have to play football. We all don't
have to play basketball.
As long as we stay true to ourselves then it
shouldn't matter and as long as we are active.
All boys come in different forms.
I wish that people will accept people that are
different and not make fun of them. This world is
filled with diverse things.
Imagine if we all did the same thing, this world
would be boring.
I am proud to say that i'm an equestrian (horse back
rider) and nobody will take that away from me. Yes,
I get thrown off but that's what it takes to be a good
rider. Yes, i know people that got kicked in the face
by a horse but they still ride.
So, if you like a sport other than football, basketball,
soccer, and golf don't be ashamed be proud.
There's nothing wrong with being different but,
there is something wrong with you not being you.
The best way of being different is being you.

BOYS DON'T CRY
Randy Luckey

*t*eardrops have been placed in my eyes
even when people think nothing's wrong
though I always try to be strong
it's hard trying to be yourself
when everyone else is looking
I try not to make a sound
be nice to have someone there when I'm down

MEN
Joshua Richardson

Don't cheer
They sit around and drink beer
Act tough
They have no fear
Every now and then shed a tear
Now I get it
It's all clear
Men are tough
Too tough to care

REPLAY
Akayla Bracey

Wake up
Skip breakfast
I don't need it
Look in the mirror
Hate what I see
Cry
Look away
Wish I could change
Go to school
Work too hard
Get a B+
Cry
B equals bad
S equals sad
How I feel
No one understands
No one
Made fun of
Hate it
Wits end
Falling apart
Cry
Starving
No food
Go run
Need to lose
Too big

REPLAY *(continued)*

Why
Why do I look like this
I ask God
I ask why?
I cry
Everyday
Every night
Every time

WHERE I'M FROM
Isaiah Daniels

I'm from blazing hot summers and
The smell of charcoal on grills
I'm from freezing cold winters
The snowy silent streets
I'm from loud and colorful Fourth of July nights
I'm from our nation's capital,
Washington, DC

5 THINGS THAT HAPPEN TO FRESHMEN
Johnajah Sullivan

They get lost
They always get asked the most questions
They don't know anyone
They can't find somewhere to sit at lunch
They don't understand that much

DAILY WORKOUT

Randy Luckey

Randy
Up
Clean
Leave
House
Bus
Train
Bus
Work
Bus
Phone
Train
Phone
Bus
Phone
Text
Facebook
Phone
Text
Facebook
Shower
Dinner
Bed

BABY GIRL
Ironelly Hernandez

I became a mother at 13
I never thought that would happen
But what could I do
Nothing
My mama told me to put the baby up for adoption
But that was not an option
There was a new life in my stomach
Regardless of my age I was going to love my baby
My mama raised me with no help from a man
And I knew if she could then I can

MY SHADOW
  Kwajuh Thomas

My shadow is me
My shadow lets me be free
My shadow follows me
My shadow is a picture of me
My shadow is a friend
My shadow is a black hole
That only I can see.

LIMERICK
  Tiffany Adams

There once was school named Ballou
Whose colors were bright gold and blue
Home of the knights
The band played that night
The other schools didn't have a clue

FAMILIA
Maya Davenport

My parents always told me to put family first
Because when you're at your lowest
And left with nothing
You'll always have a family to brush you off and
pick you back up
Because blood is thicker than water
And when your friends turn their backs
And you feel betrayed
Remember that your family will always be there
To brighten your day

MI MEJOR AMIGA
Maya Davenport

I have this one person in my life
Who I will love to my very last breath
No matter how many disagreements we may have
Not the strongest force in the world can break the bond
that we have
Because she cares about me and I care about her
And there isn't a thing that we can't tell each other
Just because we understand
We understand each others' lives and situations
We work through everything together
We have become one
She is literally my other half
Without her I would not be complete
Because there will never be another person in this crazy world
like her
I can honestly say that she can and never will be replaced
Because Enanu will be my best friend
Until the very end

BOAT
Akayla Bracey

I float and hold you
Like that fat man holds up the line
At a burger joint
In Vegas
And that waiter, so fine
You make me touch a rock
I'm sure to be torn
If I'm the Titanic
Then bring the popcorn
Because the things you have
And the stories you hold
And the laugh I hear
And the fish that go
By me
I see
Nothing
Nothing but blue
Yes, over the water
Is where I hold you

What is the What?

"And as he spoke of understanding, I looked up and saw the rainbow leap with flames of many colors."
— Black Elk

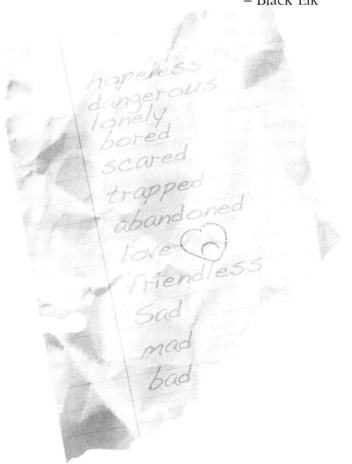

hopeless
dangerous
lonely
bored
scared
trapped
abandoned
love
friendless
sad
mad
bad

WHAT IT'S LIKE BEING DIFFERENT
Keshawn Davis-Curvey

It's hard to be different from what people expect
It's like being the only black sheep in a field of white
It's like being the new kid who never makes any
friends
It's like being the one who's constantly being bullied
It's like the day of the big test, the one you didn't
study for
It's like the feeling you get when you believe you're
doing everything right
but everyone says its wrong
It's like being the middle child, the one that craves
attention
but everyone ignores
It's like those sad commercials that come on TV
That show starving kids
That you feel sorry for
But not sorry enough to help

WHAT IT'S LIKE TO BE IN LOVE!
Johnajah Sullivan

Hugs
Kisses
Fun
Madness
Happiness
Care
Respect
Real
Hard

WHAT IT'S LIKE TO BE A BLACK GIRL
  Sha'Rell Wheeler

Cool
Funny
Brave
Intelligent
Successful
Cute
Sexy
Changing body
Acting different
Respectful
Bright
Clever
Honest

WHAT IT'S LIKE TO LIVE ON FIFTY-FIRST STREET
Armani Peoples

Fun
Loving
Dice games
Smoking
Hustling
Throwing rocks at the bus
Running from the police
Staying out late
Talking
Riding bikes
Fighting
Joaning
Having parties
Playing basketball
Playing football against other hoods
Riding dirtbikes
Up and down
51st

WHAT IT'S LIKE TO LIVE IN DC
Rebekah Newby

To live in DC, is having
The worst test score
It's eating wings with delicious mambo sauce
It's getting jumped for something as little as a coat
It's being unheard
It's getting into mischief because of boredom
It's cold winters
And very hot summers
It's shooting, stabbing and killing
It's Ben's Chilli Bowl on U street
It's like digging for gold to find that "Good School"
It's trapping and smoking just to be cool

WHAT LIFE IS LIKE IN DC
Damian Stevens

DC
Fun
DC
Diverse
DC
Exciting
DC
Dangerous
DC
My Town

THIS IS WHAT I KNOW
Kiare Ford

I know that
In this city
Where different Choppas
Like AKs spray
Where children have
No time to play
While kids go party
Their parents pray
Only to find another
Black kid lay
Dead with three holes
In his head
Like a bowling ball
Just so the police can say
'Oh my gosh, just another day.'

THIS IS WHAT I KNOW
Rebekah Newby

Tiredness
Fatigue
I wanted to sleep
Drift off into dreamland
Curl up in a ball
Grab all the covers
Feel real small
Close my eyes
But to my surprise
I'm still in class
Yawning away
Ignoring the lesson
The clock goes
Tick tock
Tick tock
It's only 9'oclock
7 hours to go
I need a cup of Joe.

THIS IS WHAT I KNOW
   Anonymous

I know how to be me
I know how to be free
I know I have no shame
And maybe I don't have game
But I'll always be the same
This is what I know
I know how to draw
And in the course of life
I'll always shoot for par.
This is what I know
I know how to cook
Anything with instructions
Otherwise, you're short
This is what I know
I know I'm a nerd
I'm artistic and smart
My favorite movie is
Paul Bart, Mall Cop

WHAT TO DO?
Tiffany Adams

What to do
When you tried and cried
all night long but no one heard
What to do
When he moved on
from you to your sister
What to do
When you prayed for the pain to go away
but it never would
What to do
When you argued til you were hoarse
cried til you had no more tears
When you finally decided to change
Leave
Figure out what to do
but your legs wouldn't move
What to do
When you think thoughts
you don't want to think
thoughts that break your heart to pieces
kill you
What to do
When all you hear
is someone telling you
He did this
She said that
Lies
Truth
What to do
When you don't know
What to do.

Haiku & Clerihew

"The gunfire around us makes it hard to hear. But the human voice is different from the other sounds. It can be heard over noises that bury everything else. Even the lowest whisper can be heard–over armies–when it's telling the truth."

–The Interpreter

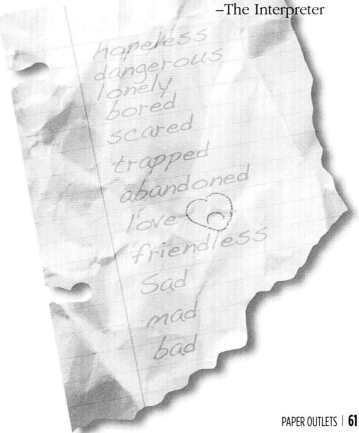

IT FLOWS
Rebekah Newby

Amazing bass flows
Bobbing my head as it goes
Steady thumping, toes

HAIKU
Joshua Richardson

Jump into the book
I'm reading about football
I play on the lines

HAIKU
Tiffany Adams

What I can do is
LAUGH DIE HATE STARE CRY PRAY THINK
But I cannot LOVE

HAIKU

Tiffany Adams

I will never love
You as much as I have done
But will always care

HAIKU

Tiffany Adams

Cry, then fall asleep
Wake up and cry more and more
Ma you don't love me

HAIKU

Tiffany Adams

Ma I'm standing here
Have you noticed lately, Ma?
I guess you haven't

HAIKU

Tiffany Adams

Do you still love me?
Will you protect me from them?
They are taking me

HAIKU

Tiffany Adams

What I ought to do
Is get an education
And achieve my goals

HAIKU

Maya Davenport

Motherless children,
Roaming alone in the dark,
Looking for some love.

HAIKU
Maya Davenport

Why is he homeless?
His story follows him round,
He has a reason.

HAIKU
Maya Davenport

The fire's hot flames,
Burn my dark brown tender skin,
It burns my childhood.

HAIKU
Maya Davenport

Smile every day,
For it lightens someone's day,
Make a difference.

HAIKU

Maya Davenport

Please have confidence,
For it will help you in life,
No one can take it.

HAIKU

Maya Davenport

A mother's love is,
So very powerful it,
Can last a life time.

HAIKU

Maya Davenport

Live your life for you,
Be a dare devil for change,
Try out some new things.

HAIKU

Maya Davenport

Crispy brown leaves fall,
Flowers bloom in the spring time,
Enjoy nature's gift.

HAIKU

Maya Davenport

Laugh, love, be happy,
Hug, Kiss, Smile, Embrace each day,
Take in the hot sun.

HAIKU

Maya Davenport

Run in the hot sun,
Enjoy the summer weather,
It's not forever.

HAIKU

Maya Davenport

Sprinklers so so wet,
Feels good against my hot skin,
I don't want to leave.

HAIKU

Maya Davenport

I'm black and I'm proud,
I know my family's roots,
I'm from Africa.

HAIKU

Maya Davenport

My family's strong,
We can fight through anything,
We have each other.

HAIKU

Lashae Hunter

Where can I go to
Escape from reality
So I can be free

HAIKU

Lashae Hunter

Playing the game of
Life where everyone wins and
Don't regret a thing

HAIKU

Lashae Hunter

I started to care
When I saw your smile but now
I have changed my mind

HAIKU
Dysis Scarlett

If you live today
You might just see tomorrow
So Live your hardest

HAIKU
Tamesha Oden

The King of the Woods
I respect you at all times
You R My Jungle

HAIKU
Tamesha Oden

I am my Mother
She is the light in My Heart
Hey U I Love U.

HAIKU 1

Keshawn Davis-Curvey

Gay, straight love don't hate
Let love be love let people
be people and live

HAIKU 2

Keshawn Davis-Curvey

When will it all end?
When will the hate stop and love
Begin? spread the love.

HAIKU 3

Keshawn Davis-Curvey

If you look in the
Dictionary for the word
Nerd, yup I'm right there

HAIKU
Keshawn Davis-Curvey

In the end, all that
Matters is my happiness
That's my goal in life

HAIKU
Kiare Ford

Gun-like resources
Is what started the tricks here
Now kids cannot stop

HAIKU
Kwajuh Thomas

Your Beautiful skin
Is brown, black, brown, black, brown, black
Just like me brown black

NOW AND THEN
Danielle Clark

Loves lost lust lately
They thieve for corrupt treasures
Broken bonds beneath

NICE COLD ARIZONA
Rebekah Newby

Cold Arizona
Beautiful perspiration
Drink, drink, gulp, swallow

HAIKU
Nelson Melgar

Beautiful Brown Girls
With great personalities
Girls are like bracelets

HAIKU

Ayanna Shingler

Trees blow in the wind
Nature's beauty is present
Air smells fresh and clean

HAIKU

Reginald Bankins

Who's the baddest boy here
Me Me Me Me Me Me Me
'Cause they can't stop Me

HAIKU

Johnajah Sullivan

When the sun goes down
Little kids run and hide 'til
The sun comes back up

ALL BLACK PEOPLE AIN'T GHETTO
Sierra Cherry

Some try, do something
Know how to prosper in life
Make something happen

HAIKU
Anthony Brent

Skinny, light blue jeans
Red Polo shirt, lookin' clean
Swag is all I need

HAIKU
Anthony Brent

I'm young and caramel
Got females, want to excel
But money got me

HAIKU
Nathan Jones

Set expectations
What's money without knowledge
Make good decisions

HAIKU
Sterling Davis

Don't be like the rest
Be true, act differently
Be Exceptional

HAIKU
Sterling Davis

It's a brand new day
My perception's different
Now that I have you

HAIKU

Sterling Davis

I'm hope, you're hatred
I will try to pray for you
So you can hope too.

HAIKU

Sterling Davis

The old me is you
I have realized it right now
That I am brand new

HAIKU

Cameron Walker

Life is like a rose
When you get close it hurts you
Great pain calms all shame

HAIKU
Cameron Walker

Sorrow is no thing
To excuse you from causing
Humanity pain

HAIKU
Cameron Walker

I sleep in a bed
When I wake I am dead inside
I cry about my life

HAIKU
Kri-Terius Jamison

The Detroit Lions
Are as strong as the Mayans
Sych, I'm just lyin'

HAIKU
Evadne Lewis

Sometimes I need my space
But you're always in my face
I need my thinking room

HAIKU
Nadja Theodore

Knowing who you are
Is knowing what is inside you
So stand tall and high

HAIKU
Donovan Barnes

I see clear blue sky
In the images I dream
My reality

HAIKU

Masaia Toran

I Hope You Learn to
Stand Up For Yourself Right Now
Before it's too late

HAIKU

Jaylahnicole Ellis

I Touch My Belly
To Feel the Movement of love
Soon, A Smile Appears

HAIKU

Nicholas Moses

People crave attention.
Try not to be like others.
Be yourself for once.

HAIKU

Nicholas Moses

Try letting it flow
Let your metaphors be cool
Feel the expression

HAIKU

Zachary Denney

I'm one of a kind
The biggest star in the sky
No one is brighter

HAIKU

Malik Peele

Flying is simple
Just throw yourself at the ground
And then you will miss

HAIKU
Malik Peele

When I was first born
I was so surprised and stunned
Didn't talk for years

HAIKU
Asia Johnson

This is what I know:
In the kitchen steaming rice,
cooking is my life

HAIKU
Donte Clayton

The ants are briskly
marching up the hill, 'til I
drown them in water

HAIKU

Zena Gbolade

This is what I know:
Talking on the phone with my
Friends is bliss.

HAIKU

Kendra Byrd

I love to be Black
Because Black is beautiful
And I love my skin

SMILE

Akayla Bracey

I like when you smile
It looks very nice on you
You should smile some more

HAIKU'
Randy Luckey

Independence Day
Marquise holds a firework
He lets go too late

HAIKU'
Randy Luckey

My sister got scared
On Halloween when I touched her
On her right shoulder

HAIKU'
Randy Luckey

Got a Playstation
For my graduation gift
In February Black is Beauty

CLERIHEW
Khadijah Chase

Soulja Boy
Is filled with joy
He went out of style
And was only on top for a while

CLERIHEW
Masaia Toran

Drake
You are a mistake
It took Lil Wayne
To bring you stardom and fame

CLERIHEW
LaKeisha Thornton

Diana Ross
You're the boss
I know you're fakin' with that long hair
But I still wanna stare

CLERIHEW

Nicholas Moses

Rick Ross
Is a fat boss
He made it to the show late
All because he's overweight

CLERIHEW

Cameron Walker

Chris Brown
You're a clown
You made Rihanna frown
And you took her down

CLERIHEW
Evadne Lewis

Rihanna
You got a whole lotta drama
Your life is spinnin' out of control
Your mess is gettin' old

CLERIHEW
Akayla Bracey

Little Miss Rihanna
Future baby mama
Hair so red, cars stop
Music so bad, jaws drop

CLERIHEW
Rebekah Newby

Drizzy Drake
I wish you'd fall in a lake
Trip and fall
With no one to call

CLERIHEW
Ava McCoy

Wendy W illiams
Think she be killin' 'em
Claims she's a woman, but I don't believe
And on top of that, she has a terrible weave

CLERIHEW
Danielle Clark

Justin Bieber
Hair chopped with a cleaver
His voice is so high
You would swear he wasn't a guy

CLERIHEW

Shalonte Pearson

Rick Ross
He says he's the boss
He has a lot of tattoos
And he looks like a fool

CLERIHEW

Reginald Bankins

LeBron James
Went to Dallas and lost four games
Jason Terry's finger is full of bling
Too bad LeBron doesn't have a ring

About the Program

Do The *Write* Thing of DC (DTWT) was incorporated in the District of Columbia as a nonprofit corporation on April 5, 2010. It received its tax exempt 501(c)(3) status from the IRS on October 14, 2011. Its mission is to promote literacy and the performing arts in young children plus provide poetry writing/publishing workshops for teens as well as college prep/lifeskills workshops and job training.

Gerald S. Nordé, Jr. is the Founder/Executive Director.

CPSIA information can be obtained at www.ICGtesting.com
Printed in the USA
LVOW091112230112

265096LV00001B/1/P

9 781930 357075